# Jam & Jerusalem

## Acknowledgements

Many thanks to the following who have published, broadcast, and in some cases commissioned various of these poems: *Exiled Writers Ink*, *Haaretz*, Harif, Ledbury Poetry Salon, *Majalla Magazine*, *Migration And Faith Communities* anthology (Hachette), *Miracle Magazine*, Peace One Day, *PN Review*, Stand With Us, Taking The Temperature (JW3), *Tipton Poetry Journal*, The Knesset, *The Jerusalem Post, The North*.

# Jam & Jerusalem
## Yvonne Green

smith|doorstop

Published 2018 by
Smith|Doorstop books
The Poetry Business
Campo House
54 Campo Lane
Sheffield S1 2EG
www.poetrybusiness.co.uk

ISBN 978-1-910367-95-7

British Library Cataloguing-in-Publication Data.
A catalogue record for this book is available from the
British Library.

Designed & Typeset by Utter
Printed and bound by CPI Group (UK) Ltd, Croydon, CR0 4YY
Cover image: Head of Catherine Lampert 2015-17, © Frank
Auerbach, courtesy Marlborough Fine Art.
Author photo: Brian Green

Smith|Doorstop is a member of Inpress,
www.inpressbooks.co.uk. Distributed by NBN International,
Airport Business Centre, 10 Thornbury Road Plymouth PL 6 7PP.

The Poetry Business receives financial support from
Arts Council England

Supported by
ARTS COUNCIL
ENGLAND

# Contents

## Diplomats

## Teachers

## Courage

## Delay

## The People Of The Book

## Jam And Jerusalem

## After Semyon Izrailevich Lipkin

*For Michael*

*Diplomats*

## Diplomats

We left none of our blood in the stones
Which you battered, bit and torched.
Our hearts are not in the leather suitcases
In which we keep the documents
Of our sojourn in your midst.
The sea of hatred which has washed you
Is tidal. There's no monopoly
On suffering, no contest, no winners.

## About Her Person

You see her as a bully,
Stiff as she moves around.

What you don't know
Is that she carries something difficult

About her person, a history
She can't talk about to herself,
Along with things she's heard.

## *Furlough*

You think it makes no sense
As you look up, walk
Across the lawn,
Your rifle shouldered.
For a moment it seems your unit's
The only place you feel at home.
As you get closer, smell your dinner,
You remember.

## Joker

Unmasked,
Every word you speak
Wears its own question.
"Joker," they say
And laugh, that always

Comes as a surprise.
If you wore make up,
Skewed your clothes,
Dyed your hair, would
The way you were heard

Be different?
The way you hear yourself,
Only on paper,
After a long time,
Unrecognisable.

Masks, jugglers, acrobats,
Clowns go home and wait
Quietly for a visit, before
Going back to work.

# Honourable Discharge

## I

What You Know Is
His nerves are shot.
Well they would be, and his mother,
Well she doesn't know what to do,
Leaves him to himself mostly.
That girlfriend of his
Hasn't been seen since March,
The good weather did it,
Off to Margate was her excuse,
He's got nothing to say on that
Or anything else.  Yes he's had
A lot to contend with,
His tours were all in Afghan,
Bomb disposal, it's a wonder
He came back at all,
Well he hasn't really
In a way.  He never goes out,
But you've got it from Mavis
That he looks shocking.


## II

Have You Heard What They're Saying?
It's easy for them
To tell your story,
Dine out on it,
When you're not there
To say different.
Bowed and broidered
Even jumped-up and kick-started
You can't go anywhere

With your eyes up from the pavement,
Thoughts unconstricted, fists unready.
All it'd take, would be to buy the story
Along with rounds of drinks
And back slaps
Unflinched over, all it'd take
Would be for you to do the shopping,
Cook something, take a bath, shave,
Open your mail, switch on the telly,
Answer the phone, share, smile, plan something,
Leave your room, stop waiting, interrogating silence.

## Shelter

She can't believe what happens,
Even with the welts on her arms
Her children mock her,
Even with the promise of escape
He rules her breath,
Deafens the promise of shelter.

## Not Afraid

A living thing
Lay on the pavement.
Someone else had trodden
On it until the stone shone red
And made other people slip.

You hadn't slipped,
But had knelt down
And put your palms out,
Tried to rub them raw.

## He Became a Criminal

When his whole family introduced him
To the craft, first it was pockets
To pick, daylight robbery.

Later he learned how to open a computer
And raid its bank accounts,
Now it's books he steals from, first

He pats them down, then after a glance,
Spits their pips onto his pencil,
Everything's unsayable.

## Risen

Silenced cobalt, copper, bauxite, amethyst, topaz
Rise like the curve of a wave, you say,
Water is the heal of your hand's cycle

From the future to the past, even while roads
Sussurate with cars so no one can hear
Any part of you, when you're buried,

Forgotten, your bones are dry, colour
Here speaks sharp as flint, soft as cub-love,
Day is paint, rain is polish.

## *When It Started to Appear*

It wore a suit and tights and always
Smelled of perfume, had a joke,
New hairstyle, wore a string of pearls.

As the years went on you aged
It didn't, but it always seemed wiser
Than you were.  When was the first time?

That you couldn't say. But the day it left,
Ah the day it left.

*Teachers*

# Change

A change would be nice,
For the women you met in Gaza
Outside the al-Basha Palace.
Where a sloe-eyed man gave you white tea
(Not tea with milk),
In a small bowl, and nothing to the others,
Except a glance which made them
Look down.
Oh better Arabic, today's Om Kalthom,
Paris sweeter, London unscathed,
The dead never dead, or at least since 9/11,
Its repercussion dead, except Saddam, Osama,
The other peddlers of terror.
Then there's politics, another tricky question
Who's good?  Shelve that for polling day,
Count your human rights,
Burn the bra (you never put back on again
The first time round), for the women, children,
Oppressed men of the hamoula.  Submit, object,
Examine, change, analyse.  Stasis suffocates.

## From Before

How is it day by day?  You know
What he's been spared, have
Bowed in shame before it.

Are very silent at this distance,
Your son was a scholar,
That's worth something.

As present and true
As a swallowed meal,
He weighs,

Walks, heavy
Inside, although
There's peace in his rest,

You remember,
Want one more moment,
Chance word from before, again.

## Gazan Bird

Fly her a long way away
While you speak at al-Basha
Where Napoleon stayed.

She knows you're from a middle class,
Have children but not so many
As to have left your body flaccid.
She can see from the computer,

The way you hold your head, speak,
Have opinions, she may have a sense of,
Or imagine your passions.

She'll never imagine how you recover
Yourself, but knows how to turn
The other cheek.  She's told you that
When she pleads with her eyes,

When her back's to the illiterate men approaching
To give you tea, her eyes say, "Don't forget me,
Talk about me at home, come back to me again."

## Inna Lisnianskaya

Inna the little finger
Of your her hand
Moves very slightly

In her lap, Lena says
Everything has a rhythm
Inside her.

She goes in and reads the news
On her computer, where yesterday
She read you her poems aloud.

They were short,
Usually two to a page,
She read them slowly,

Each one quite different.

## The Listener

What you like about him
Is he doesn't say much,
He listens to you,

To you, lets you hear yourself,
Of course you can never forget,
What you've been through

And yes, entitlement
Hangs heavy, each human has a face
More than one, well you've seen many,

The two of you,
And know who makes history,
Written not lived.

He's made it possible for you to think,
To tell him, he's made you a conversation,
Whispered, overheard, a place for thought.

# Stalker

*'Mon âme a son secret ...'* – Sonnet d'Arvers

Well so what if I do wait behind and watch
To see if you've come to work, what you're wearing,
If I can't stop talking about you, but only at home,
Because we know too many people in common?

So what if I do write to you every day with a pen
On good paper and weigh every syllable,
Imagine you as you try to make me out, as I try
To make myself out, as you never ask yourself
Exactly which one I am?

## Childhood Memories With Animals

There were birds under your shirt
Which beat tiny wings

When you were afraid.
There were sharp clawed tigers

Which pinned, needled,
And numbed your legs lame.

There were fish that slid
Along your arms so you itched.

Horses stamped
On your self-starved stomach.

Mice wriggled, crept through your hair.
Porcupines tickled your ears.

Dog-hot licks pinked your cheeks
While you were cat-ignored, invisible.

## *The Moscow River*

The Moscow River's roared at by ten lanes
Of traffic, white imperial buildings
Defy the thick air.  Candied churches
Draw head-scarved womens' chants,
Mumbled prayers, lip-pursed nods,
Finger-tip-proffered donations,
Match-tapped candles.
Fast-faced pedestrians ignore questions,
About maps but walk you blocks,
Feel the fear you guard against,
Then yield to. Moscow works hard.

## At What Price Innocence?

That's what's lost whispers a mother,
How can I protect? asks an aunt,
What replaces it? says a grandmother.
And the fathers, uncles, grandfathers
Who can't till the land, man the factories,
Go to war, wear suits, find formulae,
Be wise-women, idle. Secrets, myths unexplained.

Histories lie quieter, for now there's knowledge,
Its antithesis, webbed, processed, discussed,
Fingered, molded, but the people, children,
Strangers, who have it, have more,
They have what's always been innate, curiosity,
Questions, fear, courage, answers. They age
Living in time, informed or able to be.

## Imperatives

Throw out every idea and the books
That fostered them. Busy yourself
With practical tasks and exercises
So your mind can never idle.
Do laundry and housework daily.
Eat only home baked bread, eschew
Preserves you've not made yourself.
Follow recipes requiring maximum labour,
And the cheapest ingredients, make dresses
Cut from reusable patterns,
Which require maximal hand-sewing,
Fill your time, cultivate your garden assiduously,
Distract yourself from opinions and ideas.

## Politics

Have no place
In poetry,
Valentine Polukhina
Once said,
It dates it.
Russia's language's young,
The English left rhyme behind
Ages ago, she continued,
You're right, you're right,
About rhyme
When you translate it.
But, she went on,
Daniel Weissbort
Wrote about Brodsky,
And how he expected it
Even at sense's cost.
Ted Hughes' goal, she reminded me,
Was to preserve the foreign
In the target language.

## Beware

Beware the fisherman who counts in a shepherd's voice,
Architect who prescribes medicine, actuary who's impulsive,
Engineer who pirouettes in a ballerina's shoes,
Sloe-eyed beauty who scars her face, rider who walks,
Northerner who changes her accent, Jewess
Who changes her name, spiv who's earnest,
Clown who doesn't cry, politician who tells the truth.

*Courage*

## Courage

Cough up the outrage,
Write the only letter

Which works for you.
Breathe, wait, love-back,
Ask, try again when

Your thoughts clear.
Offer ways to say
A part of it.

# Siren

After each siren, news flash, web page,
Facebook entry, you turn to your books,
Learn Ivrit, learn it well, thank G-d
We have a land, people, language, home.

You're too old now to learn a new language
Although you're a stranger to your own,
You're too old now to translate ideas,
Pick up nuance, a refugee from thought.

How unlike Stefan Zweig, he traveled well
But gave up so young.
When you show your teeth, raise your palms,
Try not to be a friar,

Don't bow your head, or back,
Count change faster,
Read anger from raised voices,
Don't aquiesce to the shrill shrew,

No one owes you anything,
Alongside the joint-venture of statehood,
Is the treasonous free speech waived off,
As a taken-for-granted given,

While logic's defied, impossible defeated,
News refuses to stay on the screen.

## Goodbye

The front door of your mother's house closed
When you didn't understand, weren't sure, steady.

Going back's impossible, even though you don't want
The past to end, just to have more control over its limits,

And those who impose them without any sense that time
Mixed with imagination's places, and people make impatience

Which waves off even mothers who've invested everything
And fathers who love in their own image, which treads-in

The soil to leave tracks, tests it repeatedly,
Revs until the house rattles, and the teeth of all the souls

Which live there, and your heels burn, and burn
Until you've got no choice but to cool them with the breath

Of departure, to run fast, without regret, to yell the howl
Of severance, lose something then return more whole.

## Hers

Mother stand away,
Look, show that you look,
Not what you see,
Be blind, but look
For a long time,
For ever,
Be laughed at,
Stand taller than,
Bend your back,
Laugh, cry, cry but
Don't speak. Until they can,
Don't finish
Their sentences,
Cook,
Eat,
Get fat,
Lose weight,
Be slower,
Exercise,
Fail a lot and
Let them notice,
Respectfully,
Don't be their friend,
Do be their friend,
Hold them,
Don't hold them,
They'll never hold you
Completely,
Hold yourself
Always, first.

## Love List

You want him to love you
With ballet tickets, picnics,
Spontaneous theatre, not
With plans
Of where to spend the night
After a good walk, a pint.
To walk in the house,
Smile, joke, laugh with the kids
Make eye contact with you
At least once an hour. Slowly
You'll keep finding what he loses,
Touch him,
Stop asking him to feel more,
Tell you about it, not laugh
At the new car he wants to buy,
Or Tottenham's last game,
Let him and our boy swear
And talk about goal difference,
While you and our girls
Strategise their careers.
You need less,
But more in your own way,
You're both carried by
So much chemistry, age, mood,
Custom, habit, faith unbroken.

## *What?*

What would you like to know
That you can't teach yourself?

That there isn't any Other,
We're all alike, for good, for bad?

That to understand is to forgive,
In the land of the blind, the one eyed man is King,

There's never a justified call to arms?
Only failures between those who make them?

Rulers and the ruled serve and are served
By each other, or that one compromises?

That every moment is a new decision,
Everything can be changed at least in the heart?

Wings beat, land gives way,
Mountains move, valley-walls crumble-in,

Tears stop, rage quiets, pain
Finds channels, anomalies stay extant,

Rain floods, deserts writhe,
Winds ugly-smile.

You watch it all, try to speak it,
Right, wrong, change your answers,

Fix them.  You have nothing to be afraid of,
Everyone's a guide, we wear different clothes,

Eat different food, speak different languages
But they look like you, even if it's hard to see.

You can hear it you know, in our prayers,
Which ask for many different answers

From many different wisdoms and each
Maps a history and geography.

Our songs and pictures are our faces,
Maybe you'll see something there

That you'll recognize?  Not quickly,
But if you live like that

And some learn tricks this way early,
Which govern their actions so early,

That they can never change,
At least not openly,

Bide your time, step on uneven ground,
Sand shifts, grits your eye, but

Doesn't always kill.  Take water, food,
Courage, you'll understand after,

Better, it will be different,
But it will all be the same

Differences, that's all you know,
Contradictions, which can be accepted,

They're not dangerous although they feel
As though you're on uneven ground,

Tread carefully, you won't fall,
Or you will, then you'll get up,

Sunlight, rhythm, community, beyond
Don't only listen to your own heart,

But use its meter as a gauge,
Even then don't trust it blindly,

Want, know, then ask it to quieten,
It will steady you into understanding.

## *Abroad*

You never travel
It's such a strain.

Home from home's OK
For you who speak many languages,

Who still know your own
Grandparents' food,

Whose countryside looked different,
Whose cities look the same.

Could you ever write them?

## August Challenge

A special child grows up.
But what then?
Specialled as an adult?

A special child
Grows up but what then?
She disappears

If she's learned how,
And if she hasn't
She's odd, unless

She's a specialist,
Then she's allowed
To be odd

And everyone'll ignore it,
Special-cased
In a class of her own,

No comparisons,
Specialness,
Adult standard.

## *You Thank Her*

For being here for you to grow up.
For giving you time to learn

Who you are, were, will be,
In you, always.  The first person

Who'll live to 200's already been born,
It may be her, as she sits on her Parker Knoll,

Gazes at Tel Aviv's coast, thinks
Of Alexandria, where she grew up

And sailed dhows with friends
Chaperoned by her eagle-eyed brothers.

Then there is everything to her now
We've disappeared in all but name,

Become an absent interim, she's young,
A girl who dreams without responsibilities.

*Delay*

## Daddy's Girls

We all were,
There was no other way
But to burn your bra,

Be a head on a stick
Disown your body.

Now even post feminists
Are antique and girls
Go to work in lipstick,

With painted nails
Talk about their children,
As their partners man-up.

Everyone struggles equally
Or so you're told.  But you watch
Bemused she works so hard.

## It's Not Everyone Who's Interested

To hear about your parents'
Care, trials, endurance,

Limits.  How your sister's their carer,
The rest of you just help.  This

Has become a large part of your life.
Babies, work, grandchildren are common currency,

The old or sick are of less interest.
So you find who you can, employ a helper,

Enjoy the milestones, compare
What may be the illusion of being young,

A child at 60, because you've got parents,
However imperfect, who you've forgiven

And love.  Who you feel lucky to have,
Although the burden you shoulder

Is less than your sister's and their nurses
Who're so willing, but tired.

## To Wait

Why do you wait,
And what for?

You say I use my pencil
To listen

For questions
With no answer

In the white evening which echoes silent,
Waits for safe arrival from a place

That's not needed anymore,
Which loses nothing by its absence.

## Delay

Look, there are things you have to do
But first you just pick up an ink pen,
Yes, a real one and see what's there
To keep you back from the chemist,
Bank, dog, house, stewing last night's meat.
What frees you in your bed when everyone's on the move,
Talks about things, is on the lookout,
Everything's here, books leap onto your screen

Without you having to move a muscle.
Is there anyone else in the same position
In the adolescence of a bedroom,
Disguise of a study, compass of a work station,
Aura of an office, curtilage of a kitchen
With a mind that hovers over a pen's dance?

## The Unspoken Illness

The unspoken illness is on everyone's lips
But nobody wears the label, it's time
To talk about the number of people who come to you
Because they know, and judged you after your
Post natal depression, because time has shown,
Time alone, that you've lived some sort of life.

It's time to wear labels, bi-polar, schizophrenic,
Anxiety-disordered, instead of neurotic, hysterical,
Depressed.  Time to find causes not results, time
To neutralize not judge.  Taboo and its place shift
How to eat, take rest, sustain family, limit power,
Protect property, curb greed, settle disputes,

Doesn't need drama, but myth does.
The myth which worries at unfaceable distinction, deformity,
Conformity devises systems which not everyone can/
Should use ever/always/sometimes. It's time to wear labels,
Offer them to others, not when they approach you at night,
(Oh everyone sees each other clearly enough then), met

Disrupted, slid along, asked soft or angry questions of,
In a stream which might give, not split, even though
The stitches become open lattice, like the wire on a suspension bridge.
You've learned to teach your children, they're better than you,
They never double stitch their seams, now it's time
To learn how to learn from outsiders who visit what you say,
You'll never see them, but you'll hear yourself.

# Landscape

Your favourite landscape's
A cleaned house, fresh linen,
A fridge full of food
Someone else's cooked
Who you've stirred the pot for.
This isn't the West's vision

Or one of undoubted privilege,
Other things come into it,
You want it known.  Mothers,
Grandmothers, daughters, sisters,
That it's more than a room of your own
Lets you write.

## Overheard

Someone outside's using
A drill,
Then knocking on wood.
A car door slams,
Footsteps hurry,
An engine starts,
A car drives past,
Two people sing,
You catch a few phrases.

## Rainy House

In order to smoke
You put on his shoes
And a thick robe
Over your nightie,
Lay a towel
On the camping chair,
On the flat roof
Outside your bedroom,
Light up, smoke yourself sick.

## Herzelia's Big Desk 1

Nabokov worked at a desk,
He told Lionel Trilling,
In his youth this hadn't
Been his custom.

The big desk, office chair,
Wrap-around verandah,
Pink bougainvillea,
Is somewhere important work
Can be done.

## *Herzelia's Big Desk 2*

"Write it like prose,"
Ruth Fainlight said,
"Lineate later.
I like propelling pencils."

"Never think about writing
Unless you're doing it,"
Alan Sillitoe eventually said,
When you asked and asked
About being a writer.

## Herzelia's Big Desk 3

So what's important?
The soul or the part you call
The you that's private?
Before and beyond words.
You try to name it,
Or give a name
To everything but the it
That urges you away,
From the rub.

*The People Of The Book*

## Terms

"B'sha tova," for someone pregnant,
"Long life," at shivas,
"Only simchas," at burials,
"Please G-d by you," to unmarrieds
At weddings, "Shabbat shalom," on shabberses,
"Gmar khatima tova," from Rosh Hashana
To Yom Kippur, then "well over the fast,"
"Kasher ver sameakh," on Pessakh, then
"Khanooka sameakh," "tubishvat higiya,"

You're not robbed of your own voice,
But opened.  Then some speak, others
Make space to hear/invite/help/empathise,
Some just greet, but echo throughout.

# Rosh Khodesh
### (Orach Khayim 418-424)

The jewels women wouldn't surrender
For the Golden Calf, they volunteered
For the Tabernacle, first consecrated

On Rosh Khodesh Nissan, as the moon
Rose again. You take stock each month,
Say tehillim at Shacharit, add the solemn
To the festive.

## Shtum

Baked khallas, built succahs, forgiven fasts, eaten enemies,
Entertained family, visited friends, exhausted conversation,
Returned-to poems, prayers, texts as beautified as Lisbon
Bibles (25 good years to go?) forgotten anti Jew marchers.
Our friends comfort us, worried, angrier than we allow
Ourselves to be, more outspoken. But it's our enemies we
Watch dumb, then conjecture, in here we talk but not outside,
Outside we keep shtum.

# Bedeken

He wanted a wife, this man,
Who has so many friends, a family.
He bought his wedding shoes years ago,
Wore them in in his bedroom,
Then walked towards her.
Knew the secret word
They'd agreed on,
No one else ever would,
Though they'll both speak
A language we can hear.

## Four Corners 1

Sharp-edged, hospital-bed-neat, defined, reciteable, immutable,
Her four corners bind freedom, an internal courtyard full of
Food smells, a place to fly away from on a Qum mesmerised
By patterns, freed by cool air, mind's distances.
"Orzu!, Orzu!", guests chant, "Handa! Handa!" they whoop.
Custom waits for a bride who doesn't understand what's being
Folded away, has no words for it.

## Four Corners 2

Not her, there's nowhere she can't go,
Be listened to, although

There are hollows under her eyes
That look like sadness, she wonders why

No one tells her what to do or think,
Her views are so distinct,

She wears her clothes like they're tailor made,
Eats carefully, afraid

To lose her athletic figure, not for vanity,
Rather because exercise after work's her sanity,

No one's more modern, unconstrained, but somehow
She always stays after a row,

Her children turn their backs, judge her in silence,
She's too much of a success, trained to the recompense,

She notices almost nothing, when there's no meal left
For her next to the bills, notes, diary's heft,

She looks for someone to tell about her day
When her family punish her as they turn away,

Her husband, less successful than he should have been,
Folds up on his side of the bed so he can't be seen.

## Four Corners 3

Thumb tip to flattened palm,
Little finger stretched up in alarm,

A square of terror blocks out the light,
Breaks hold, disables her from the fight,

Her squared hand, the ache in her spine
The lock of her knees, the silence of the mime,

And why why always so passive never clenched
Into a fist? Why why ask herself questions,

Before she acts, checks off her list? The dilemma's fork,
Conundrum's arc, circle squared, the can we talk?

What would be so wrong in answering back,
Wrong or right, unfiltered this or that,

When did she learn to be so measured,
When everyone else was so self-assured?

Whoever told her it wasn't her turn
Until she was too old to learn?

Thumb tip to flattened palm,
Little finger stretched to contain the alarm.

## *Four Corners 4*

Geometric, symmetrical, closed,
All answers known,
Flat, unencumbered,
Angles neatly numbered,

The page's done its work,
No one's been hurt,
It slips into a drawer
Without any goal,

The place for you to speak,
Then keep your peace,
To wipe over then forget
The what if, the yet.

# Towards Language

Yours is not theirs,
The tenement Yiddish you've borrowed
Came from the fire escapes

New York apartments dropped
In "West Side Story",
A Yiddish which London's Jews

Told punch-lines in, you laughed
But never understood.
Your mother tongues spanned

Continents, histories, recipes, fights,
And silenced you until Grammar school
Began to name your thoughts,

For decades you've written for someone
Other than yourself overheard,
Now your plate's empty.

## Bikur Kholim

Your mother used to sit like this
While you'd rest, she'd suck her teeth,
Sigh, "ach yarab", break away
Bustle in the kitchen,
Come back, clink a teaspoon
Against a china cup,
She never took sugar,
But always gave you some
If you'd co-operate,
She'd wait, was patient,
Her patience was special.
Your flip-a-lid visits,
Were different to your post natal,
Lets-make-you-comfy-so-you-don't
Flip-your-lid visits, or the
Something's-wrong-with-your-body-
Keep-you-cheerful visits.
But it was always food, well meant.
Off-your-food? Tsoyi khavasonak?
"Can I make you something you fancy, or soup"
(Always chicken broth, easy to digest),
"Water? Soup is better."
Doctors she said were well meaning,
Important, not always right,
Certainly not in everything,
"You need people to get better –
Hospital? Someone,
Has to sit with you there,
Day and night,
You never know – must read the charts,
Check, listen, dress nicely, smile, sleep
In a chair, bring the nurses Quality Street,"
She never thought the irritation

Of being ill and supervised, not left
To get on with it alone, would be
The thing anyone would want,
Bikur kholim, was foisted on you,
That's where you saw life, lived it, wordless,
For ages, when you seemed still, looked blank,
Confused your untrained self,
In your family, where the flip-your-lid's understood,
Everyone knows what to do, but has no
Language for it,
They pretend like it's not happening,
Or there's no danger, no end notes,
Let the moment pass. Look-after you well,
Joke or mock,
Try to shock you out of your absence,
Being khoonook,
Having gone goom, chapa, lakhbakh,
Moody, broken down, depressed, irrational.
She waited to mend, colour your visits bright.
Take you out of the shadows,
Brought quiet angels, invited the manic to visit the unipolar,
The old, the young, the well, the ill. Wheeled them into her sun,
Warmed their blood, cooked so the smell of food visited
The unhungry, who remembered the smell of her food,
Knew it, were too ill to eat.

## The People Of The Book

Whoever thought
That would mean so much?
That pages would be replaced
And paper poems would,
Like ink, become obsolete?

People of the word, who ever knew
That the naming of things would be absorbed
Into so many media, invisibly transmitted?
That beyond the crass and cruel,
Libraries would open, uncensored

In photocopied pages
Complete with thumbprints
Around whose peripheries you'd read
Without ever having to leave your bed.

*Jam And Jerusalem*

## A Soldier's Scribe

This job frightens you.
You listened to him this year.
Heard mortars in his quiet voice,
Saw death in his dark eyes,
Smelled fear on his even breath,

This job frightens you because
You've known other soldiers
From Europe, Africa,
The Far and Middle East, Asia,
And because victims raised you.

This job shames you,
You're his aunt,
Watch him hurt, cynical,
Afraid, frustrated, human,

He tolls like a bell hung from canons
Trapped in headstock, driven by gudgeons,
Begs for silence you can't give him,
Or his children.

## The Farhud

We walked on Shabbat
In the Bustan al-Khass
(Lettuce orchards)
On the East bank
Of The Dijla (The Tigris),

Or in al-Saa'doun, built
To look like Hyde Park.
Watch us work, prosper, plod
Tread the middle ground during
A two thousand six hundred year
Sojourn with family, food, festivals.

Listen to us speak Aramaic, Qiltu,
Then Gilit. You never learned
Our languages after you arrived,
We wrote literatures preserved
For you now in different geographies.

Watch Britain's renegade Grand Mufti

Translate National Socialism into
His Promised-Land apartheid, listen
To the whispers that the Führer
Was born in an Egyptian village.

Watch him and hundreds of Palestinian
And Syrian intellectuals-in-exile train soldiers,
Police, militia-men and children, watch
Nothing stops the Golden Square Generals,
Even once their leaders temporal and spiritual
Run away from the British, for whose oil-fuelled
Infantry eight kilometers was further than the walk

From Ambassador Cornwallis' dinner plate
To his card table.

Look, there's a man in a dark suit at Maqbra,
Who'll later press his cheek and arms up
Against a semi-cylindrical grave where
One hundred and eighty Farhud-dead are buried.
This is not the only tomb, they were not the only dead.

But go back before the Omer, watch us
Tremble as we asked "Mnein Jitem"
That Erev Pessakh after the lawyer,
Rashid al-Gaylani's coup turned
The hilleq bitter.  Watch our hopes surge
When within the month he and the Grand Mufti
Escape from the British to Iran, plummet
When Yunis al-Sab'awi declares
Himself Governor General and orders us
Penned in our homes, soar again when it's he
Who's deported within the day. Hear us attest

To our treble-terror reprieved when we eat
Our Tbit on the Shabbat which runs
Into Tikkun Leyl, and hear Regent
Abd al-Illah's due back the next day,
Sunday June 1st. Watch us cheer him home
On the first day of Eid al Ziyarah.

Then watch soldiers, police, civilians attack us
On al-Khurr bridge, at al-Rusafa, Abu-Sifain
Everywhere until 3 a.m. and silence. Watch
At 6 a.m. on the second day of khag when
They start again.  Not just the poor from al-Karkh

Who cross the river empty handed,
Then load-up having cruelly sacked

Our homes, shops, synagogues,
But from everywhere they yelp

"Idhbahu al-Yehud" (butcher the Jews).
Drilled by Salah al-Din as-Sabbagh,
Or by centuries of knowing our place,
Keeping the rules, paying the price
Being no guarantee of protection.

They cut up Jewish babies and threw them
Into the undertow, no Moses survived.

They raped girls and old women,
Cut their breasts, no Dina survived.

They beheaded and severed, taunted
And tore. Dragged Jews from buses
Which they used to run them over.
Every attack intended to humiliate.

The dead, hurt, stolen, destroyed
Uncountable, even once the Regent
Called in the cut that felled
The saturnine mob. Where was natural,
Civil, military, sharia law? The assumed
Duty to dhimmi?

In the stand taken by Moslems
Like Dr Sa'ib Shawkat,
Dean of Baghdad's Medical College.
In the acts of landlords
Who risked their lives to save those
Whose houses the Hitler Youth-styled
Futuwwa had painted with red khamsas.

In the arms of neighbours
Who caught children in blankets
When they were thrown to safety
And sheltered families who jumped
Across flat roofs where Baghdad
Used to spend its summer nights.

Yes, we fought back, we boiled
Siraj (sesame oil) and threw it
From our shnashil (latticed balconies)
Where women, unseen, had watched
Their households' comings and goings.
We used the bricks from our parapets,
We had no guns, few had iron fists.

Since the funerals our children
Remember with new knowledge
And their picnics of beith-bla'ham,
Timman-ahmar, and kahi never go south
To al-Kifl for the pilgrimage, sing
Shirit Khagvarim at its seven
Waystations, or hear the tomb
Of Yehezkel cry for its Jews.

## Jam and Jerusalem

*After Alan Brownjohn's 'What's The Music For?'*

Explain to the confused, trickle-sweet polite-nod cattle-prod
Confused, what's implied? City divided, population enraged,
Rights maintained? For whom, in what idiom, with which
Boundaries? Old hack, buy-backs options, futures sutured,
Susurrated with amnesia, the low hum of expedience
In the face of our dead, un-blamed in the name of

Not-my-hemisphere, the age-old won't-fight-back
Rocking-Jew-calm, the alleged tiny-colonied Jew-army or
Oil pipes, Gertrude Bell, T. E. Lawrence, F.O. stud-blood
Orientalists, anti-Jewify ralliers too late for Golders Green,
Manorial waste the 13th century gave the godded Godyere's
Temple fortuned knights whose plunder-improved now-Anglican

Domain, houses Jew and gentile un-torched or torching
For now. Oh writer-descendants of Ducksetter Lane's
Knights of St. John, Jerusalem the Golden's traders,
Craftsmen, scholars, rabbis would have come to you,
Their treasure, Torers, Mishners, Talmuds, tephillin,
Unchanged. Explain, didn't those Jewish turn-the-other-cheek,

Abraham-washed feet in ancient times ask of the Godyere
Pastures a welcome for us, once they came to understand?
Do you see footsteps in this hundred years' war? It will eat
A lot of grazing cattle, metal armour, hoisted banners, boiled
Blood, rejected refugees, stabbed civilians, before it
Iron Domes itself. Explain, don't leave yourselves out
Of another chapter which we shall write.

## Hundred Years' War

This is the most important moment
In the last fifteen years and the next eighty-five
And you exoticise repression,
Enjoy opera about benign supremacists
Interspersed with elegant picnics, course by course
Reassured over champagne, insulated.
This is the most important moment

In the last fifteen years and the next
Eighty-five and over and over again you reason,
That and that and that would be enough
To make me into a terrorist, as though
You can explain, relieve, own the mayhem
With reason, transform it by your act
Of imposed, assumed humanity.

In Iran the bloggers say you in the West
Fail to grasp the double glance of their leaders,
Westward, Eastward, for you, for them,
And lift sanctions with a focus on ISIL while Syria,
Yemen, Gaza, Lebanon don't fit
The puzzle – it's untidy but paying for their boys
To die doesn't seem to confuse you.

There are no similes, metaphors, strophes
That whistle in the trees under the Glyndebourne
Which shades you, there's no silence either
In my bowed head or when I try to hold my back
Straight.  My children live in impossible times
And run amok as children do, their fears are masked
In where they'll work, who they'll love, not a lot is said

About before war came explosions instead of the war games
They play on consoles, it's impossible now
They're old enough to sense that we'll grow away from the front
If we're as lucky as we've been so far, although
We remember our parents' wounds, oh oh tell me
When to speak, write, when to stay silent, how to teach
The when to pray, hold faith, take up arms.

## 'All Poets Are Jews' – Marina Tsvetaeva

So defend us, silent English sisters, brothers,
The taste of our names is growing bitter in our own mouths.
We're sore with the sojourn, we'd thought to have settled.
Computers have been the latest channel for the oldest
Of calumnies to become currency while no one noticed

They'd been given an old script to act, to pixilate
For caressed touch-screens, lapped laptops, smarter phones.
Hooked, lined, sinkered, throttled, piled in a rotted basket
So many of us turn up silent palms, make inane jokes,
Huddle in communities, love, self-hate, identify, differentiate,

Practice, atheise, agnosticise, intellectualise, new, old, scholastic,
Theistic, ideas. Oh, oh that we, like Israelis, could just be,
Rather than spend so much of our time, because you force us to,
Trying to understand ourselves, to explain, justify, not as an exercise,
Like our Sages, Rabbeyim, Tannayim, but as an apologia.

Not in my name. What is my name? History's not this, that,
Other, whatever it is it's everyone's, we see what's demanded,
Done, shown – now in a new language with old declensions,
Years ago you heard its whisper, felt its breath on your skin,
Abstracted because it was something you were supposed

Not to notice. Do poets notice? Where are your lines?
Aren't you going to say anything at all? Why's that?
Will screens, Kindle, blogs, films broadcasted record you?
See, hear, divine the latest scree put on your steep path.
Will we be alone again?

## Now The Rhetoric

Now the rhetoric begins to cloud us prepared by music
Rhythmed by fear, hypnotised, rat-a-tatted, rocked back and
Forth. "Strike the heart of the kaffir." Again and
Again the exhortation, "What does that country have
For you now the caliphate's been declared?" And with
Promises, inducement, veiled and asserted threat, again men,
Dictators, sadists, power-crazed, blood-eyed history wakes
Up its limp excuse for a way forward while Darfur seeks
A woman President to do things differently, find a new way.
A small hand slices above the head while heads are
Severed, the rule of law, custom, ritual, are bled of heat. G-d
The judge, ventriloquised by murderers who silence with guns,
Knives, hands, households, fear, the spill of words, while
You think, mine, love, invest-life. The road forward/back's
Moaned about, reasoned, mocked, ignored. It won't be
Newspapers that bring you through, radios which link your
Arms, these have failed you, made you commerce, trained
Your base faculties, left you as stunned as the rhetoric,
As dumb. The fumbled, ungrammatic web offers to answer
Your search, forays, with voyeuristic curios, to teach you
To be more human, forget the births of war, bleed the
Richer soil of tailored news which smells the past in rain,
Heat-bake cracked, ooze-crumbled. Fleshes government,
Grains choices, nursed industry, toddled ventures.
Mother/daughter/grand-daughter shared corridors of
Power, sistered/brothered, eye-watched, old men retired
For a generation, rite-of-passaged, trained to reason, kept
Pink-of-foot, ritualised, reminded, loved, fed, not allowed
To hunt for food, made to plant, harvest, surrender their tools
At the hearth. This and no less calls. Could be seen.

## You Won't Apologise

Because not enough have died,
We've paid already in the West where we burned,
In the East where we were made to leave all we had,
Humble ourselves, collude, knowing, unknowing,
Until our own earth threw itself in our faces.
We aren't occupiers, we spend our boys and girls
To buffer our state, you won't apologise for 66
Or 5,777 years of survival, you won't lie down, shut up,
Be ashamed for your neighbour who wants
To break down your door and that of your reglionist's,
Co-descendents, his, or those he suspects wherever they live,
Women, children, oppressed sons of the hamoula
We stand for all the same things, forget the side shows
You know to be absurd. Live, work, whisper, pray, yell,
Call, email, ask your children to.  Powers wilt for
Lack of oxygen, breathe with you so as they atrophy
We'll be prepared to bake bread, make salad, wash babies,
Harvest our own crops.

## The Jews Of Paris

Left in hoards, by foot, in cars, on trains,
My father among them, took a bicycle
From the hundreds abandoned at the station,
Strapped it to the back of the goods carriage,
Terrified his mother as he left them,
At each of the endless stops in sidings, cities,
Towns, villages. He'd disappear, pedal
As his blood pumped, return with baguette,
Sausage, cheese, fruit, water.

Four days it took
To get to St Porquet,
Where they registered
With the Mairie, as Jews,
Were Red Cross billeted,
But only after my father,
Aged sixteen, disembarked,
Lay on the concrete platform,
Stomach down, "I slept for twelve hours,"
He says, "My mother waited until I woke up,
With my younger brother, Joe, on the bench,
She hadn't left her seat on the train since Paris,
She was too afraid even to go to the toilet.
When we arrived she understood me.
It was the gendarmes who rounded us up
From Mme Delshay, our billet.
Took us to Gurs, they ran it.
There was no Gestapo involved.
There was no electricity, running water,
We slept in open sheds,
Boys were taken from there at 2 a.m.
To diesel cattle trucks,
The rattle of their engines fuelled

The headlights they trained from
One to another in the freezing February
1942 Pyrenees. They screamed like stuck pigs
Because where they'd slept on the earth,
Eaten and defecated in the same buckets,
Was a safer hell than going out of France, to work
In Germany." British from Boukhara, my father
Asked to see the Chef de Gendarme,
Said over and over again that he and
His brother were Prisoners Of War,
According to the Geneva Convention,
Something he'd heard Canadians talk about
On the train there. They were taken to St Denis
And interned, with their father Pinchas Mammon (z'l),
Via Pau, where my father says, "They put us in hotels,
It was a dream, we ate, had hot baths,
St. Denis wasn't bad" he says
"Some of my female cousins
Were at Drancy,
It was more dangerous to be outside,
Some were De Gaulle's secretaries in exile,
The Germans kept the rules.
They barked at the French on the Paris platform,
Why have you brought the women,
[My mother included] and children?
We only asked you for the men,
We put mother on the train back to St Porquet,
She'd never been alone in her life, spoke no French,
Saw her husband and surviving sons taken off to St. Denis.
It was a medieval castle whose thick walls have disappeared,
As for Darquier's Gurs, no one talks about it."

## Poetry In The Pogroms

When do Mumbai, Toulouse, Belgium,
Paris, Norway, Manchester become Pogroms?
What's critical mass?  Look around,
No neighbours you'll say.  Individuals.
Extremists.  Not us.  What about
All the other places in the world
Where they're killing people?
The other holocausts?
There are no other holocausts
But there's a monopoly of suffering.
Don't speak. Think, read, quietly pack,
Teach those who'll listen,
That we've moved before, they have a choice,
To end their sojourn or hide here
Among the embers of tolerance
Which can't protect them.

## Fight Back

Here on your soil, we aren't protected.
Laws, neighbours we all embrace,
Will fail us or succeed, protect or fail to.
We're no different to anyone else,
But we're a target which knows the form,
Our grandparents, parents, their friends knew,

Had heard, seen, felt and either
Told us with silence, myth or toothless old mouths,
Or by not knowing things because their parents
Had been too dead to teach them,
Their grandparents, because feelings were outlawed.
As a way to get through we were trained

To point-duty without knowing its name, face,
The purpose it had for us, oh you'll say
They're not loyal, we look away, move,
But understand, want to separate you from
The bloodshed of defending us, ourselves
From the shame of not being defended.

Memory, not history, flaws not fault,
Humanity's deaths in the absence of duty,
Law turned away from fictions espoused,
Murderousness appeased, while its functionaries
Are made marks.  Cut cut cut like a swordsman
Always after the banner-carrier's led the charge,

Cut cut cut on the hashish pipes around which
All the promises snaked which planned
The latest round of deaths, cut cut cut
As everyone defies the latest news
Intended to strike fear in the enemies
Of its protagnists, cut cut cut until the era

Gets tired and meanwhile yes there are starving,
Drenched, parched, diseased places which want
Or take piecemeal aid, intervention which baffles
People who know the chop
Of full scale war, unstoppable sewers of blood.

Degree, measure is everything but who sues
For peace before a war that's decade-revived?
Who understands leaders whose generations
Outlive Hitler, Stalin, Mao?
Who knows what language to speak while
The Tower of Babel's engineers fall daily

Their hod-carriers beg
Not to climb the scaffold? What talks to all
Lost and extant beliefs that point
To the supremacist, watches with open eyes
As you lie down, rise up, walk by the way,
Observe so you can't say you didn't see.

## St James's Church Piccadilly 2013/14

In Israel walls have always wailed,
Attracted cruelty, stupidity,
The homeless, destitute, righteous-dead,
Have always been trampled-over, ignored,
Hatred removed our shoes with ancient ignorance.

In Israel wails have always been evoked
By neighbours who knew, loved, hated us,
Envied our similarities, our differences,
You do nothing new, you wheelers of history,
Aren't you ashamed to be teaching lies
To people who've paid their dues and believe
Or have nothing to believe in, who've looked
To you, learned, been taught, shown.
What have you shown them this season but hate,
What have you done but stoked ancient suspicion?

Israel's neighbours are bathed in blood, repress,
Mutilate their girls, flatten their breasts,
Overfeed them for early puberty, marriage,
Sew them apart from men.

These indignities you're silent about,
While children have no rights, not even to food,
Unless they show fealty.  These indignities
You're silent about, the butchers of Syria, demeanors
Of Egypt, you don't react to Darfur death watchers,
The decades-murdered Christians of the Middle East,
Your own homeless you don't house, yet grin your pride on YouTube,
We're dumb-struck, feel word-silent, unlanguaged, invisible,
But gasp the unexhalable, the disenfranchisement of the hunted.
What we need to feel is rejection, there's no room for a clever,
Reasoned response.  Only rejection not terror in our hearts.

Only rejection greater than the Islamist terror will impress,
Where is your part in this? Witness the abuse of the Christian
On YouTube who tried to explain at St James's why
Christians were wrong, he was abused, called a Jew.
What then? Where are the words, gestures answers?
Almighty show us another way in our halls of worship
We can't be silence, we mustn't be.

## *Thursday 19th November 2015*

In South Tel Aviv a 36 year old Palestinian
Stabs an Israeli praying, because he's a Jew

Praying. This isn't different to Isisian violence
Although it's called rage, reasons are implied,

Absolve him of responsibility, make him
A victim. Those who kill a hundred

In Paris are perpetrators. These old tropes
Suffer labour pains, give birth to death,

Feed black milk to babies.
Do you want us to write the future

With the weather vane of the past,
Can you see a new direction, take us with you?

*After Semyon Izrailevich Lipkin*

## Early Summer

We lost the Battalion's seal
While loading up to get out of Jolly's farm
We'd already been replaced there,
And the Command weren't Russian anymore.

Remington semi-automatics still rattled
As we set up a table under a cherry tree.
The Battalion Commander grinned,
"God bailed us out today",

And Nikita Ivanovich, our (Party) Instructor,
Knitted his blond brow
At the Manych river, which shone like a blade
Still warm with blood.

Could he, abandoned by faith
Understand what's worse, the sea's loss,
The roar of the red-grey water,
Or the echoes of German curses?

So much that was bitter had risen that night.
What could the dawn promise him?
The militant sparkle of the river,
Early summer flowers?

Sarcasm twisted his lips
His clear mind shined in his eyes,
His features were refined by fear.

Oh Instructor Nikita Romashenko
If only you'd survived to see
The suffocation, fear and pain.
Now in early summer's sweet air

I feel deaf to German cannon,
And foreign languages,
But threatened again by people
Who reject the rule of law.

I wait stupefied for the fated end,
Only one thought haunts me,
That I must bury my fear deep
And my smile is ugly.


1949

## Evening In Lykhny

I remember the tender bell
Of Abkhazia's Compline,
And the eucalyptus' sleep
Overhung by leaves
That caress the air,
The smell of grapes
And the golden fingernail
Of the young moon.
I remember the warble
Of the nightingale
In early spring,
When April clamped a flute
Between its lips.
I remember the slender-waisted
Grey elders I met,
As Dioskurian verse chimed,
Then trailed off.

# Moonlight

City boys use probes
To look for bread from nightfall
Until the Turkish sabre moon,
Which lights up the peasant families,
Pales over the steppe's shacks,
Everyone will be sent to Kotovsk in an hour,
Then Kazakhstan's regions,
"They'll be liquidated as a class."
In red wagons
They'll become insomniacs,
Who'll mourn
Truth corrupted –
The grass stands proud against the wind, bows,
Stretches to the sea.
This sullen, silenced, weakened people
Are guarded, if one girl goes to the toilet,
Everyone troops behind her, the door's left open,
No one runs if everyone's in sight –
I remember the steppe bathed in moonlight
And the deafness of human grief.
I meet a retired friend in Odessa,
He's old now,
Didn't escape his fate,
Spent eighteen years in Siberia.
Does he remember dispossessing the kulaks
Who probed for grain?
The breeze that unfurled
The blades of grass, the
Moonlight that used to shine.


1963

## *You Appeared To Me In My Home Town*

In 1920 I thought I saw you
At the Church of the Assumption.
I thought you came
Round the corner
Of a Ukrainian village
With a child conceived in hunger.
When your beauty shone
Like a golden queen
On the windows of the Chartres Cathedral
I looked into your face
And wondered if you knew
How soon your son would be crucified.
When you were at Kazan
And didn't cross the Lake
Where ice and waves colluded
But crossed the Neva's front line
With your boy to share the blockade's bread.
When you were the Sistine Madonna,
It seemed to us you had two wings
And were invisible as you flew towards us,
Kept flying until we came to life, lived, live on.


1987

## Autumn At The Sea

A deserted beach, sun-lit flare-gleamed waves,
Bright sand, tired obese fishermen,
Chatty white shirt-fronted seagulls,
A black pack of thin dogs.

The fishermen have grown women's breasts.
Where did all the mackerel and flounder go?
Odessa's elderly play goat,
And chat on sunbeds,

I share their fate,
Know nothing as fresh
As their questioning lilt,
Their grammar's irony.

A boy argued with southern poverty,
Left home fast, found nothing
When he replaced the sea,
Learned nothing, nothing.

How did I get here, in whose wake,
Where did I scatter the salt of reason?
Life, what shall I do with you,
What shall I do with your simple pain?

I came back so late, when the waves were cold,
Barely swam, was beached on a thick, dark shore.


1982

# On The River Istra

It's not the stars that praise themselves,
As they glow on holy eve –
But gentle angels
Who put candles at the feet of the Mother of God.
And when starlight descends
On Palm week
It doesn't find a derelict garage,
An empty village,
But the abbey garden which has disappeared.
Sweet apples will ripen by the bushel,
Giant loaves will be racked out for sale,
There'll be honey jars and butter pats
Thrown up in a sloboda.
Near the fine-cloth factory.
The merry river Istra's
Seven-belled-hum won't change.
The eternal Virgin will see the nuns
Who work in the garden, who spread the canvas,
She'll choose a bride for her son
Who met the world from a stable.


1986

## In The Field Behind The Forest

Going into the fields with a blade of grass,
A flower's stalk.
I'm not a flower but a princess,
Who wears a crown not a wreath.
I've made a contribution to the monastery's coffers,
Am one of the retired who left the world
Been condemned to be creatures of field and forest.
We'd lived, with joy, in cloisters,
Glad of the land's blessing,
But the world breathed with the plague of sickness
Threatened, reprieved.
Marinushka's road was paved one way,
Annushka's another.
Where's the princess now?
She's just a thin petal
Who believes we'll cure one another.
The Easter water's close,
We'll bake forty larks
For forty martyrs,
And even though I've become grass
We're together, together again,
We're not ill with plague, or ruined.
I call, "Is that you, Marinushka,
Are you there Annushka?"
While only the aspen weeps over me,
Only earth, flowers, grass surround me.


1985

## Ghosts

We'll magnify our leaders' portraits,
Make solemn declarations,
Churn out landscapes as decreed.
Hacks, amateurs,
The untalented,
I'm one of you, I'm yours.

We, who knew what was wrong
Are condemned to the shame
Of our miserable fate.
Our capital idles,
We're still the hapless boys
God wanted us to be.

We're unknown ghosts, whose work
Doesn't make printed reviews.
Unbroken though bent,
Barely awake to God,
We write

About those who gasp,
Weighted-down
With tears and shame,
Stuck in the mud
Of self reproach,
But who persist

And tell Russia
That only we are the living,
For our sins.

1957

## I Hear Them

They carry quarried sand,
I wake up, go to my window,
The pale-grey birch
Looks into my room,

The bright sky shines so blue.
What broke the silence?
Horror's knowledge
Penetrates the heart's dark bulk.

Did they dig the quarry only for us,
Did we lie down there alone?
Didn't Mother Russia soothe me,
Cry when the ground did?


1956

## Nomadic Fire

We've lived in this empire
For over four centuries,
Its interruptions breathe at us
With birches and nightingales.
We used to be poor, threadbare
Highway inn-keepers
Who rushed to battle-fronts and barracks,
But none of that served us.
We wasted time senselessly
Both when the Nile insisted
Leviticus use and extend
Hellenic speech and numbers,
And when poet-clothed Spain
Rose in prayer
As the grandee Talmud Torer
Excommunicated Spinoza from the Temple.
What is our destiny,
Will our hunters let us rest?
Or are we nomadic fire,
Eternal, formless?
Where should we light ourselves now,
Take our footsteps?
In whose torches should we burn,
Whose fireplaces should we warm?


1973

# Glossary

## Anglicised Hebrew

*Simchas* p. 62
Celebrations of the cycle of life.

## Arabic

*Dhimmi* p. 79
A tenet of Sharia Law dating from the seventh century to the present which accords freedom of religion together with protection from persecution to Jews and Christians living from the Atlantic Ocean to Central Asia, *Dhimmi* status is granted in exchange for acceptance of Muslim supremacy to varying degrees which accord with the demands of the ruling sect.

## Biblical Hebrew

*Bikur Kholim* p. 71
Visiting the sick. In this poem the concept's reversed, the patient visits to be healed.

*Khag* p. 78
Festival

*Khalla* p. 64.
A type of bread eaten on the Jewish Sabbath.

*Merzuzer* p. 81
A parchment inscribed with Deuteronomy 6:4 encased and attached to the right doorposts of a Jewish house.

*Mishners* p. 81
The first major written redaction of the Jewish oral traditions known as the "Oral Torah". It is also the first major work of Rabbinic literature.

*Omer* p. 78
The counting of seven weeks between the Jewish Festivals of Passover and Pentecost.

*Pessakh* p. 62 & 78
Passover

*Rabbeyim* p. 84.
Plural of Rabbis.

*Rosh Khodesh* p. 63
New Moon, The Jewish lunar calendar has 12 months, 13 in a leap year.

*Rosh Hashana* p. 62
Jewish New Year

*Shacharit* p. 63
Morning Jewish Prayers

*Shiva* p. 62
The seven days of mourning observed by deceased's mother, father, son, daughter, brother or sister. During which the currency of which they are at home to visitors who wish to condole or care for them.

*Succah* p. 64
A temporary building with its roof loosely thatched, used for meals during the Jewish festival of Tabernacles.

*Talmuds* p. 81
The body of Jewish civil and ceremonial law and legend comprising the Mishner and the Gemara. There are two versions of the Talmud: the Babylonian Talmud (which dates from the 5th century AD but includes earlier material) and the earlier Jerusalem Talmud.

*Tannayim* p. 84
Scholars of old. From the Hebrew meaning to give [knowledge].

*Tehillim* p. 63
Selection of psalms recited daily but customary for women to gather on Rosh Khodesh (see above) to say as a group.

*Tephillin* p. 81
Jewish phylacteries.

*Torers* p. 81
Five books of Moses in a scroll and used in synagogues (aka Torah).

*Yom Kippur* p. 62
Day of Atonement.


## Egyptian Arabic

*Ach Yarab* p. 71
Onomatopoeic word for a sigh


## Judaio-Arabic, Iraqui

*Beith Bla'ham* p. 80
Meat and potato fritters.

*Hilleq* p. 78
Another word for kharoset (Hebrew) which is a sweet, dark-colored paste made of fruits and nuts eaten at the Passover Seder.

*Kahi* p. 80
A deep fried sweet pastry.

*Mnein Jitem* p. 78
Where did you come from?

*Shirit Khagvarim* p. 80
Song of men (literal).

*Tbit* p. 78
A slow baked Sabbath dish of stuffed chicken and rice.

*Timman-ahmar* p. 80
Iraqi dish of chicken and rice.


## Judaio-Tajik

*Chapa* p. 72
Being silently angry.

*Gone goom* p. 72
Shut down. Stuck in a sulk, silent.

*Handa* p. 66
Laugh.

*Khoonook* p. 72
Lacklustre.

*Lakhbakh* p. 72
Without motivation/lazy.

*Orzu* p. 66
Concupiscence.

*Tsoyi khavasonak* p. 71
Something you fancy eating.


## Modern Hebrew

*B'sha tova* p. 62
[May the baby arrive] at the right time. Said to someone in
preference to congratulations.

*Khanooka sameakh* p. 62
Happy Khanooka. Said on the 8 days of the Festival of Lights.

*Friar* p. *41*
Pushover.

*Gmar Khatima Tova* p. *62*
May you be [judged favourably and] written in the Book O Life.
Greeting when you meet somebody between the Jewish New Year
and Day of Atonement.

*Kasher ve sameakh* p. *62*
Greeting between people during Passover, it means kosher and
happy [a festival], at this time where the dietary laws are stricter
than usual, leavened foods and their derivatives being excluded.

*Shabbat Shalom* p. *62*
Greeting said on Shabbat when you meet somebody.

*Tikun Leyl* p. *74*
1st night of the Jewish Festival of Shabuot (Pentacost), when
people stay up and learn Jewish studies all night to commemorate
Moses receiving the Tablets of Stone on Mount Sinai.

*Tubishvat higiya* p. *62*
The announcement of and greeting of the annual tree planting
festival which also commemorates the trees new yield. This occurs
on the 15th of the Jewish lunar month of Shevat.

*z'l* p. *88*
Zichron Levracha – Of blesséd memory – said after the name of
someone who's passed away.

## Yiddish

*Bedeken* p. *65*
Bridal veiling. As a result of the biblical story of Rachael and Leah,
a Jewish groom veils his bride prior to the ceremony only after she
speaks a private word to him which he recognizes.

*Shtum* p. *64*
Quiet.

# Notes

*Fight Back*  p. 90
Arab Spring – Egypt – 17th December 2010, Libya February 2011

*Inna Lisnianskaya*  p. 27
Inna Lisnianskaya (1928–2012) – Semyon Izrailevich Lipkin's widow. https://biblio.wiki/wiki/Main_Page

https://pen.org/essay/cold-war-dress-code-remembering-inna-lisnyanskaya

*Politics*  p. 34
Brodsky – From Russian With Love. https://www.amazon.com/Russian-Love-Poetica-Daniel-Weissbort/dp/0856463426

*Shtum*  p. 64
In 1482 the first Jewish bible published in book form.

www.bl.uk/learning/cult/sacredbooks/religiousbooks/.../biblelisbon/lisbonbible.html

Jews were expelled 25 years later.

Anti-Jewifiers relates to the rally scheduled to be held in Golders Green in 2015 but which was moved to Westminster https://www.theguardian.com/world/2015/jul/04/london-anti-jewification-demo-dwarfed-by-anti-fascist-counter-protest

*The Farhud*  p. 77
The Farhud occurred on the 1st and 2nd June 1941 on the Jewish Festival of Shabuot (Pentecost). This poem was commissioned by Harif/Stand With Us for the commemoration of the 75th Anniversary of The Farhud. The author read the poem on the 2nd June 2017 at a service at Lauderdale Road Synagogue. She read it at the Israeli Knesset (Parliament) in Jerusalem on the 6th June 2017 to mark the Government's announcement that they would compensate victims on the same scale as Holocaust survivors.

*St James's Church Piccadilly 2013/14*  p. 92
https://londonist.com/2013/12/bethlehem-unwrapped-visit-the-wall-at-st-jamess-piccadilly

UNICEF reported that despite the fact female genital mutilation (FGM) is illegal in Egypt, 87% of Egyptian females between 15 and 49 have suffered FGM.  In Somalia the figure is 98%.

*Lykhny*  p. 98
Lykhny – Abkhaz village, known for its beauty and ancient history from as early as 6 A.D.

Compline – Final church service of the day.

*Moonlight*  p. 99
Kotovsk – A major railway station on the Odessa to Zhmerinka line, in the Ukraine's Oblast of Odessa.

"They'll be liquidated as a class." – A Soviet slogan for the Kulak's fate.

*You Appeared To Me In My Home Town*  p. 100
Church of the Assumption – Moscow's Russian Orthodox Cathedral (aka the Cathedral of the Dormition).

Kazan – Leningrad (now St Petersburg)'s "Our Lady of Kazan" Cathedral.

Where ice and waves colluded – during WW2 there was only one escape route from besieged Leningrad over the ice of Lake Ladoga which became known as "The Ice Road to Salvation."

Neva – A river in northwestern Russia which flows through the western part of the Oblast of Leningrad.

It seemed to us – The subject pronoun here refers to Lipkin and his wife, Inna Lisnianskaya, who was baptised by her nanny as an Orthodox Christian. Her mother was Christian Orthodox and her father was Jewish.

*Autumn At The Sea*  p. 101
Goat – Play dominoes (colloq.).

*On the River Istra* p. 102
Sloboda – A tsarist Russian free trade zone.

*In the Field Behind the Forest* p. 103
Marinushka – Diminutive for Marina Tsvetaeva, whom according to Daniel Weissbort's wife, Valentina Polukhina (Professor Emeritus of Russian at Warwick), visited on her return from exile when many others gave her a wide berth.

Annushka – Diminutive for Anna Akhmatova, Lipkin's close friend.

We'll bake forty larks – The Russian Orthodox bake lark pie for Easter.

Together, together – Lipkin, a Jew, felt empathy for all faiths, to quote his widow Lisnianskaya, "He loved those who understood deity – was above them," i.e. who didn't feel supreme.

*Ghosts* p. 104
I'm yours – But see Alexander Solzhenitsyn, "... outstanding poets existed almost imperceptibly, noiselessly, in the literary world. They were little known for decades, because they didn't rush to serve regimes, as almost all other members of the poet coterie did. Semyon Lipkin and his wife, Inna Lisnianskaya were part of this phenomenon ..." ('Novy Mir Moscow, No4, 1998) and "A Close Reading of Semyon Izrailevich Lipkin by Solzhenitsyn, Green and Makarov" (forthcoming from Smith|Doorstop).

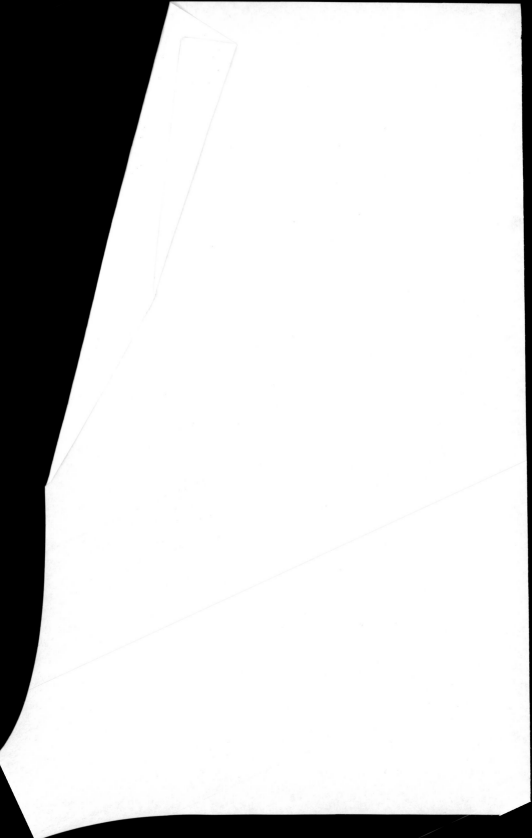